The Voice and Spiritual Education

by Hiram Corson

PREFATORY NOTE

While it is the purpose of this little book to emphasize the importance of vocal culture in its relations to literary and general culture, it is not its purpose, except incidentally, to impart elocutionary instruction. Attention is called to a few features of the subject, which, if realized in any voice, would contribute much to the technical part, at least, of good reading.

Special stress is laid upon the importance of spiritual education as the end toward which all education should be directed, and as an indispensable condition of interpretative reading. Such education is demanded for responding to, and assimilating, the informing life of any product of literary genius; without it, mere vocal training avails little or nothing. By the spiritual I mean man's essential, absolute being; and I include in the term the emotional, the susceptible or impressible, the sympathetic, the instinctive, the intuitive,--in short, the whole domain of the non-intellectual, the non-discursive.

With the kind permission of the editor, I have embodied in the part of the book devoted to the voice, my article on Vocal Culture, published 'The Atlantic Monthly' for June, 1895.

H. C. Cascadilla Cottage, Ithaca, N. Y., 30 Jan., 1896.

THE VOICE AND SPIRITUAL EDUCATION

Can reading be taught? is a question often asked, and partly for the reason, it may be, that so many readers who have gone through courses of vocal training in schools of elocution, or under private teachers, so frequently offend people of taste and culture by an extravagance of expression, by mimetic gesture, and by offensive mannerisms of various kinds. But a reasonable inference cannot be drawn from such readers that vocal training must necessarily do more harm than good.

Yes, much can be taught, and is taught, and well taught, it may be; the desideratum is the education, intellectual and spiritual, especially the latter, without which the mere teaching and training are vain and impotent.

The organs of speech can be brought by intelligent training into a complete obedience to the will and the feelings; and without this obedience of his vocal organs, a reader, whatever be his other qualifications, cannot do his best. He is in the position of a musical performer who has sympathetically assimilated the composition he is rendering, but whose instrument is badly out of tune. A reader may have the fullest possible appreciation of the subject matter, intellectual and spiritual, of a poem, and a susceptibility to all the subtlest elements of effect involved in its form; but if he have not full control of his vocal faculties, he can but imperfectly reveal through his voice, his appreciation and susceptibility. This control can be secured only by long and intelligent training. The voices, generally, of even the most cultivated people, have gone more or less astray, and need to be brought back from the error of their ways, before they can serve effectively to interpret a literary product.

Many great poets have written subtly organic verse, who could not vocally realize its potentialities, they not having their organs of speech sufficiently under control. Samuel Taylor Coleridge is an example. 'Amongst Coleridge's accomplishments,' says De Quincey, alluding, in his 'Literary Reminiscences' to Coleridge's lectures on Poetry and the Fine Arts, at the Royal Institution, 'good reading was not one; he had neither voice, nor management of voice.' But he must imaginatively have heard the wonderful verse of Christabel and Kubla Khan, as an organic, inseparable part of the poetical expression. Mere literary skill could not have produced such verse. It was a texture woven by the spirit, which he could not adequately exhibit to the physical ear, as he was not master of the physical means for so doing.

To read naturally is a common and a very vague phrase. The question is, what is nature? It is the object of the science and art of reading, to realize as fully as possible the imperfectly realized instincts of the voice. 'There is a power in science which searches, discovers, amplifies, and completes, and which all the strength of spontaneous effort can never reach.'

When people speak of the natural in expression, they generally mean nature on the plane on which they are best acquainted with it--the plane of common speech. But the language of the higher poetry, or of tragedy, or even of impassioned prose, is, more or less, an idealized language, for the expression of which a corresponding idealization of voice is demanded. To read, for example, Milton's apostrophe to Light, at the beginning of the third book of Paradise Lost, after the manner of common speech, would be somewhat absurd. The idealization of voice demanded for the reading of such language, is not, however, a departure from nature, but is nature on a higher plane.

'Enter into the spirit of what you read, read naturally, and you will read well,' is about the sum and substance of what Archbishop Whateley teaches on the subject, in his 'Elements of Rhetoric.' Similar advice might with equal propriety be given to a clumsy, stiff-jointed clodhopper in regard to dancing: 'Enter into the spirit of the dance, dance naturally, and you will dance well.' The more he might enter into the spirit of the dance, the more he might emphasize his stiff-jointedness and his clodhopperishness.

Of this distinguished advocate of 'natural' reading and speaking, Mr. Grant, writing in 1835, says: 'Oratory is not his forte, ... he goes through his addresses in so clumsy and inanimate a way that noble lords at once come to the conclusion that nothing so befits him as unbroken silence. He speaks in so low a tone as to be inaudible to those who are any distance from him. And not only is his voice low in its tones, but it is unpleasant from its monotony. In his manner there is not a particle of life or spirit. You would fancy his grace to be half asleep while speaking. You see so little appearance of consciousness about him that you can hardly help doubting whether his legs will support him until he has finished his address.'

The writer of this justly says of the Archbishop's writings: 'They abound with evidences of profound thought, varied knowledge, great mental acuteness, and superior powers of reasoning.' But his 'natural' theory in regard to speaking, did not, it appears, avail with him, even when backed by such abilities.

'Nature,' says the Archbishop, 'or custom, which is a second nature, suggests spontaneously the different modes of giving expression to different thoughts, feelings, and designs, which are present to the mind of any one who, without study, is speaking in earnest his own sentiments. Then, if this be the case, why not leave nature to do her own work? Impress but the mind fully with the sentiments, etc., to be uttered; withdraw the attention from the sound, and fix it on the sense; and nature, or habit, will spontaneously suggest the proper delivery.'

Such instruction as this is not unlike that which Hamlet gives to Guildenstern, for playing upon a pipe, and would be, in the majority of cases, hardly more efficacious: 'Govern these ventages with your fingers and thumb, give it breath with your mouth, and it will discourse most excellent music. Look you, these are the stops.' Guildenstern replies: 'But these cannot I command to any utterance of harmony; I have not the skill.' The last sentence tells the whole story. The Archbishop, with all his great abilities, had not the requisite skill in oratorical delivery.

So this may be said to be the conclusion of the whole matter: the main result which can be secured in teaching reading, and in training the voice, is technique and elocutionary skill of various kinds--a skill which the student can bring into his service, when voicing his intellectual appreciation and spiritual assimilation of a poem or any other form of spiritualized thought; the illumination of the subject-matter, intellectual and spiritual, must come from the being of the reader. He can't give to his hearers what he doesn't possess. The saying of Madame de Savigne 'Il faut, si l'on veut para 頬 re,' is applicable to the reader. An attempt to express what is beyond the range of his spiritual life and experience, at once betrays his deficiency. And no amount of mere vocal training will compensate for this deficiency.

There are two unwarrantable assumptions in what Dr. Whateley writes about Elocution: 1. That a reader or speaker can do with an untrained voice what his mind wills, or his feelings impel him, to do. Not one in a thousand can. 2. That all principles of Elocution which may be taught will continue in the consciousness of the reader or speaker--that he will be ever thinking of the vocal functions which he exercises. 'The reader's attention,' he says, 'being fixed on his own voice, the inevitable consequence would be that he would betray more or less his studied and artificial delivery.'

All true culture, to be true, must be unconscious of the processes which induced it. But before it is attained, one must be more or less 'under the law,' until he become a law to himself, and do spontaneously and unconsciously what he once had to do consciously, and with effort.

It may be that Dr. Whateley's views in regard to Elocution were somewhat the reactionary product of the highly artificial style of pulpit oratory which appears to have been the fashion in the Dublin of his day. (Note 1.) He was a man of such perfect honesty and integrity, with such a resulting aversion to sham and empty display of every kind, that he came to regard all training in vocal delivery as unfavorable to genuineness. His theory was fully confirmed, he may have felt, by some of the popular theatrical preachers around him, who made a display of themselves, and who, in the Archbishop's words, 'aimed at nothing, and--hit it.'

When I was a small boy, at school, sixty years ago, all the scholars had to read aloud twice a day; the several classes standing while they read, and toeing a chalk line. The books used were the New Testament and Lindley Murray's English Reader. The standard instruction imparted was very limited, but very good so far as it went, namely, 'Speak distinctly and mind your stops.' Each boy read, at a time, but a single verse of the New Testament, or a single paragraph of the English Reader; the 'master' himself first reading a verse, or a paragraph, each time the reading went around the class.

Well, the result was that all the boys acquired at least a distinct articulation and a fluent utterance, properly sectioned off by their minding the stops. Some of the boys, of whom I was one, had to read aloud, at home, from other books. When I showed by my expression, or, rather, by my want of it, that I did not understand what I was reading, I was at once told so, the passage was explained and read to me, and I had to read it again, to show that I had caught the meaning and the proper expression. If I were required to read something which was entirely new to me, my eye was exercised in running ahead of my voice, and taking in what was coming, to the extent of a sentence or two, in order to read with sufficient expression not to be stopped, as I was very impatient of interruption, especially if I particularly enjoyed the subject-matter.

When I look back upon these daily exercises in reading, at school and at home, I feel that nothing could have been better at the time. There was no such thing as 'speaking a piece,' with gesture, 'limbs all going like a telegraph in motion,' and straining after effect. It was simply careful, honest reading, with no attempt at make-believe of feeling. No encouragement was given to any affectation of that kind; but whatever impressed my listeners as genuine feeling and appreciation on my part, was duly praised; and I was very fond of praise, and was stimulated by it to do my best.

I fear that such reading has very much gone out of use, and that untimely technical instruction has taken its place. Call on a college student to read any prose passage extempore, and what is the result in ninety-nine cases out of a hundred? Why, he will read it, experto credite, in a most bungling way, with an imperfect articulation, without any proper grouping or perspective; and if the passage be an involved and long-suspended period, which his eye should run along and grasp as a whole, in advance of his voice, he will be lost in it before he get half way through it. He has had little or no practice in reading aloud. He has 'parsed' much in the lower schools, but his parsing has not resulted in synthesis (which should be the sole object of all analysis), has not resulted in a knowledge of language as a living organism, and the consequence is that his extempore vocalization of the passage is more or less chaotic and--afflicting.

Extempore reading requires that the eye be well trained to keep ahead of the voice, and to take in a whole period, or a whole stanza, in order that each part of it be read with reference to the whole, that is, with the proper perspective. To do this demands an almost immediate synthetic grasp, the result of much training.

The perspective of speech is virtually a part of the meaning. One who reads without perspective does not give his hearers the exact meaning, for the reason that, subordinate parts standing out as prominently as leading parts, the hearer does not get a correct impression of their various degrees of importance, unless he do for himself what the reader should do; and, certainly, not many hearers are equal to this--not one in a thousand. Our estimates of all things are more or less relative, so that perspective plays a large part in whatever we take account of. What would a picture be without perspective? But it is of equal importance, of greater importance, indeed, in the vocal presentation of language.

A true perspective demands, on the part of the reader, the nicest sense of the relative values of successive and involved groups or sections of thought-- those belonging to the main current of thought being brought to the front with a fulness of expression, and the subordinate groups or sections according to their several degrees of subordination, being thrown back with a corresponding reduction of expression. Along with this, the whole must have that toning which reveals the spirit of the whole. Could there be any better test than reading, of a student's knowledge of the organic structure of the language, and the extent to which the thought is spiritualized? Hardly. The ordinary examinations of the schools, through questions, are wholly inadequate for getting at such knowledge--for evoking a student's sense of the life of the language as an organ of the intellectual and the spiritual.

Technical knowledge is a good thing in its way, but a knowledge of life, in whatever form, is a far better thing. And it is only life that can awaken life. Technical knowledge, by itself, is only dry bones. The technical, indeed, cannot by itself be appreciated. It must be appreciated as an expression of life--as an expression of the plastic spirit of thought and feeling.

Reading must supply all the deficiencies of written or printed language. It must give life to the letter. How comparatively little is addressed to the eye, in print or manuscript, of what has to be addressed to the ear by a reader! There are no indications of tone, quality of voice, inflection, pitch, time, or any other of the vocal functions demanded for a full intellectual and spiritual interpretation. A poem is not truly a poem until it is voiced by an accomplished reader who has adequately assimilated it--in whom it has, to some extent, been born again, according to his individual spiritual constitution and experiences. The potentialities, so to speak, of the printed poem, must be vocally realized. What Shelley, in his lines 'To a Lady, with a Guitar,' says of what the revealings of the instrument depend upon, may be said, with equal truth, of the revealings of every true poem; it will not tell To those who cannot question well The spirit that inhabits it; It talks according to the wit Of its companions; and no more Is heard than has been felt before,' by those who endeavor to get at its secrets. Good reading is a vocal manifestation of responsiveness, on the part of the reader, to the hieroglyphic letter.

Such early training in reading as I have described, is the best preparation for the more elaborate expression demanded by the higher literature. And we shall not have a true, honest vocal interpretation of literature until we return to this early honest reading. I say 'return,' for, so far as my knowledge goes, there is a plentiful lack of it, at present, in primary schools--a lack somewhat due, no doubt, to the ever-increasing amount and variety of knowledge which students are compelled to acquire in the schools. There is no time left for education. He would be the ideal teacher who could induce a maximum amount of education on the basis of a minimum amount of acquirement. But just the reverse prevails. Acquirement is made the all in all, and education is left to take care of itself. The acquisition of knowledge, too, becomes a mere indulgence with thousands of people, in these days--an indulgence which renders them more and more averse to any of that independent activity of mind upon which education so largely depends.

I am quite surprised at what M. Ernest Legouv says, in his 'Petit Trait de lecture ?haute voix l'usage des primaires,' of the importance attached, in America, to reading aloud. In the very opening sentence of this work, he says, 'La lecture haute voix compte, en Amerique, parmi les plus importants de l'instruction publique; elle est une des bases de l'enseignement primaire.' And elsewhere he calls upon the people of France to imitate the United States of North America, in making the art of reading aloud the very corner-stone of public education! Where could M. Legouv?have got this remarkable opinion of the high estimate, in this country, of reading aloud, as an educational agency? From whatever source he derived it, it is certainly most remote from the truth. What Sir Henry Taylor says of the neglect of the art of reading in England (Correspondence, edited by Professor Dowden, p. 225), is quite applicable to this country. After saying that he regards the reading of Shakespeare to boys and girls, if it be well read and they are apt, 'as carrying with it a deeper cultivation than anything else which can be done to cultivate them,' he adds, 'I often think how strange it is that amongst all the efforts which are made in these times to teach young people everything that is to be known, from the cedar of Lebanon to the hyssop on the wall, the one thing omitted is teaching them to read. At present, to be sure, it is a very rare thing to find any one who can teach it; but it is an art which might be propagated from the few to the many with great rapidity, if a due appreciation of it were to become current. The rage for lecturing would be a more reasonable rage if that were taught in lectures which can be conveyed only by voice and utterance, and not by books.'

Here, by the way, is indicated what the literary lecture should be. It is a comparatively easy thing to lecture about literary products and to deal out literary knowledge of various kinds, and cheap philosophy in regard to the relations of literature to time and place. A professor of literature might do this respectably well without much knowledge of the literature itself. But what students especially need is to be brought into direct relationship with literature in its essential, absolute character; so that the very highest form of literary lecturing is interpretative reading. Such reading brings home to sufficiently susceptible students what cannot be lectured about--namely, the intellectually indefinite element of a literary product. Much of what is otherwise done for students, in the way of lecturing, they could do quite as well for themselves.

'A book of criticism,' says Hume, 'ought to consist chiefly of quotations.' The same should be said of a literary lecture, with the important addition to the word 'quotations,' 'effectively read.'

To return from this digression, what seemed so strange to Sir Henry Taylor, is not so strange when it is considered that the dealing out of knowledge, in the schools, on the part of the teacher, and the acquiring of it on the part of students, leave no time for education of any kind except the little which is incident upon the imparting and the acquisition of various kinds of knowledge 'from the cedar of Lebanon to the hyssop on the wall.'

Perhaps the greatest danger to which education proper will be more and more exposed, in the future, will be the great increase of knowledge, in every department of thought. This may sound paradoxical; but with the increase of knowledge, the temptation will correspondingly increase to make the acquisition of the greatest possible amount of it, in schools, colleges, and universities, the leading aim. To give the student the fullest command of his faculties, should certainly be the prime object, to which the acquisition of knowledge should be subservient; but this object seems to be more and more lost sight of, while to cram his mind to the utmost, with vague, indefinite, and heterogeneous knowledge, is getting more and more to be, if not the sole, at any rate the chief, consideration. This state of things prevails from our lowest to our highest schools. We hear and read ad nauseam that the word 'education' means 'a drawing out.' This one etymology everybody knows, if he doesn't know any other. Lecturers and writers on education, and school circulars, keep reiterating it. There are certain truths so ding-donged in our ears that they lose all their vitality. One of these certainly is, that the word 'education' means 'a drawing out.' Sometimes a teacher at a school institute, after presenting this etymology, proceeds to present what he considers the best methods of ramming in!

There are schools, and their patrons think them excellent, which out-herod Herod in their slaughter of the Innocents. Sad, indeed, is it that the young are so debarred, as they are, by the tasks imposed upon them, from all sweet and quickening 'impressions before the letter.' 'As in Hood's exquisite parody of George Robins's advertisement,' says George Henry Lewes in his novel, Ranthorpe, 'the pump is enumerated as having "a handle within reach of the smallest child," so do our illustrious educators wish to place the pump of knowledge within reach of the meanest capacity, that infants may forego the mother's milk to drink of its Pierian spring.' The time must come, it is no doubt in the very far future,--there are no indications, at present, of its being in the near future,--when it will be a pedagogical question how to induce a maximum amount of education with a minimum amount of brain-slaughter.

To get back, now, to the leading subject, vocal culture: a college student whose voice was neglected in early life, and, worst of all, whose sympathies were not then so attuned to good literature, by the influences and atmosphere of his home, that he came to have an inward impulsion to vocalize whatever he specially enjoyed in his reading, will not be much profited by a course in soulless elocutionary spouting. One may have an extraordinary natural gift of vocal expression which is superior to all adverse circumstances; but such an one is a rara avis in terris. Unless there be an early initiation into literature and its vocalization, in advance of the benumbing technical instruction of the schools, much cannot be expected from the great majority of students, in a literary or elocutionary direction. Truly 'illuminative reading,' to use Carlyle's phrase, is, apart from this condition, quite out of the question.

In the whole range of linguistic and literary studies, English, Latin, Greek, German, French, Italian, Spanish, or whatever be the language and literature studied, vocalization should be made of prime importance. So it should even in Anglo-Saxon and early English studies. When I conducted these studies, which I did, for more than twenty-five years, I pronounced to my classes all that was gone over. Beowulf I read to them entire. The interest of students in this Anglo-Saxon epic is much enhanced when it is fluently and vigorously read. It is the only way by which the spirit of the poem can be brought home to them.

To know Chaucer as a poet, and not merely as a writer of fourteenth-century English, his verse, which, after a lapse of five hundred years, continues to rank with the best in the literature, must be voiced; and to voice it, with the best knowledge of its pronunciation which has been attained to by Alexander J. Ellis, in his 'Early English Pronunciation,' and by other phonologists, requires a careful training of the voice and much practice. A susceptible reader comes, in time, to feel, to some extent, what the intonation, also, of the verse, must have been. To inspire students with a permanent interest in 'the morning star of song,' the teacher must be an accomplished reader of his verse, and must train his students to the best reading of it of which they are capable. Of course, a knowledge of the language in its historical development, previous to Chaucer, is desirable, though not indispensable, to appreciate his poetry; but the best vocalization, in the fullest sense of the word, which can be attained to, is indispensable. To know of what earlier inflection any final -e is the residual, is well enough; but I cannot think that any one would insist that such knowledge is indispensable to an appreciation of the poetry. Philology is not the handmaid to poetical cultivation. She can be dismissed altogether from service. There are no emergencies, even, where it is necessary to engage her temporarily.

In the study of Latin and Greek, even with our imperfect knowledge of the ancient pronunciation, and our no knowledge of the ancient intonation, of these languages, it is all important that the student should read Greek and Roman authors aloud. A student who has first been trained to read Greek and Latin prose with fluency and expression can then have considerable appreciation of verse in advance of any technical knowledge. And if he be trained to read in time, he will know what 'quantity' really means. As Latin and Greek verse is read in the schools (when it is read at all), it is accentual, not quantitative. I cannot think that there was any more quantity in Greek and Latin than there is in English, or in any other modern language, unless the

Greeks and Romans spoke more in time than we do, which is not likely. The Romans were probably more measured in their speech than the Greeks. Syllables, in Greek and Latin verse, must have been made long or short by an intoning of the verse.

When Vergil, or Ovid, or any hexameter poet, is read in the schools, his verse is the same as that of Longfellow's Evangeline, made up of xa, ax, and axx feet. (Note 2.)

The following verse from Ovid, for example (Met. I. 143),

Sanguine | aque ma | nu crepi | tantia | concutit | arma,

is read in the same way as the following from Longfellow's Evangeline:

Or by the | owl, as he | greeted the | moon with de|moniac | laughter;

and the first and second of the following verses from Ovid (Met. I. 148, 149),

Filius | ante di|em patri|os in|quirit in | annos. Victa ja|cet Pie|tas; et | Virgo | c 鎰 e ma-|dentes Ultima coelestum terras Astr � reliquit,

are read in the same way as the following from Evangeline:

And as she | gazed from the | window she | saw se|renely the | moon pass Forth from the | folds of a | cloud, and | one star | follow her | footsteps.

Ovid's Met. I. 22,

Nam coe|lo ter|ras et | terris | abscidit | undas,

is read in the same way as Colossians iii. 19:

Husbands, | love your | wives, and | be not | bitter a|gainst them;

and Ovid's Met. I. 36,

Tum freta | diffun | di, rapi|disque tum | escere | ventis,

is read in the same way as Psalm ii. 1:

Why do the | heathen | rage, and the | people im|agine a | vain thing.

Rebus sic stantibus, what's the use of talking about quantitative and accentual verse, as if they were really two kinds of verse? They are, to be sure, but they are not made so, in reading.

There is, in fact, no such thing as a spondee in ordinary speech. A true spondee must be made by voicing two syllables in equal time, and each without stress.

After having been trained in the 'scanning' of the schools (counting verses on the fingers), I threw aside and tried, and successfully tried, to forget all the scholarship of Latin verse, and began reading Vergil aloud and in time. I felt, at first, the movement of the verse backward, the ultimate and the penultimate foot came out first to my feelings; and in time, the movement of the entire verse became distinct.

Chaucer's verse must be read more in time than modern verse. (Note 3.) But all true verse must be read more in time than prose. And even impassioned prose, like some of De Quincey's, for example, must be read, more or less, in time. Perhaps it may be said that both prose and verse should be read in time according as the thought is spiritualized.

The choruses in Milton's Samson Agonistes can be properly appreciated only when read in time. The verse has been condemned by some critics, as if Milton, whose ear, as De Quincey says, was angelic, could not compose good verse when he dictated, in his blindness (to which the merit of the verse of the Paradise Lost and the Paradise Regained, was, no doubt, somewhat due), this last of his great poetic compositions!

Even in the study of modern languages, in the schools, there is not enough pronouncing of the original. It is mostly read off in English. If a teacher of a foreign language, whose pronunciation is correct (if it is not correct, he should not teach it), were simply to read aloud to his students, they having the text before their eyes, and were to require them to read, until they could pronounce correctly and fluently, the language studied, it would be a much better introduction to the language than the usual grammatical grind at the outset. A certain amount of grammatical grind is necessary, but a thorough training in pronunciation should come first of all. And then, if a student got nothing other than a good pronunciation, it would be certainly worth more to him than any amount of grammatical drill without it. A living language should not be studied scientifically until it is known. And the most important thing to know, at first, is its pronunciation.

Thomas Elwood, Milton's young Quaker friend, tells us, in his autobiography, of his reading Latin to the blind poet,--how he was required to get rid of his English pronunciation of the language, which his 'master' disliked, and to learn what he calls 'the foreign pronunciation,' his description thereof showing it to have been the Italian,--and then adds, 'Having a curious ear' (that is, a careful, accurate, nice, keenly susceptible ear), 'he understood by my tone, when I understood what I read, and when I did not; and accordingly would stop me, examine me, and open up the most difficult passages to me.'

This sentence suggests that much more might be done than is done, in the way of getting at students' appreciation of the Latin or Greek they may be reciting, by requiring them to voice the original in advance of translating. After having attained, by sufficient practice, an easy fluency of utterance, they could--or some could--bring out, through their voices, much which they could not reveal through translation or any amount of exegesis. All the members of the class might be on a par, so far as translation and exegesis go, in exhibiting their knowledge and appreciation of the original; but there would always be a few who could reveal through vocalization what is beyond translation and exegesis. And the professor would not necessarily need to have the 'curious ear' of a Milton to detect this kind of superiority of the few.

This brings me to say that, in literary examinations, whatever other means be employed, a sufficiently qualified teacher could arrive at a nicer and more certain estimate of what a student has appropriated, both intellectually and spiritually, of a literary product, or any portion of a literary product, by requiring him to read it, than he could arrive at through any amount of catechising. The requisite vocal cultivation on the part of the student is, of course, presumed.

But even an uncultivated voice would reveal appreciation, or the want of it, to some extent. For, after all, it is not so much the cultivated voice as spiritual appreciation, which tells in reading. I have heard 'poor, but honest' voices read some poems very effectively, and I have heard rich, but dishonest voices read very afflictingly. To adapt the French saying, le style, c'est l'homme, it may be said that la lecture haute voix c'est l'homme. Reading reveals the reader's spiritual appreciation or the absence of it. And it is only to the extent that a reader assures his hearers that he has himself experienced the sentiments to which he gives utterance, that he impresses them. To one who has truly appreciated it, there is nothing more dreary than the usual elocutionary rendering of a poem.

Suppose a teacher were to examine a student on such a poem as Coleridge's Christabel by questioning him about it, and the student were to show that he was thoroughly acquainted with all the facts and details of the poem; there would still be no evidence of that student's susceptibility to what in the poem constitutes its mysterious charm,--none whatever. The student might be utterly destitute of such susceptibility, and yet he could just as well prepare himself to answer all the teacher's questions. A very small boy might do so, whose appreciation of poetry had not gone beyond 'How doth the little busy bee.' There might be a most susceptible literary genius in the class, who might fall below the other student in such an examination! It is quite likely that he would, for he would be chiefly occupied with the poem as a poem, and would assimilate its life without retaining a recollection of all the details, to which the other had given exclusive attention. Or suppose the poem were Gray's Elegy written in a Country Churchyard, and the student were to pass a perfectly satisfactory examination thereupon, on the basis, say, of the valuable notes in Professor Hales's Longer English Poems; what would that signify, in comparison with the reading of the poem, which would unmistakably show whether he had responded, to any extent, or not, to its sweet evening pensiveness, to the general tenor of the theme, to the moulding spirit of the whole?

That he should understand the articulating thought, all the grammatical constructions (and there are several which need to be particularly looked into), and all points to which attention is called in Professor Hales's notes, is, to be sure, important; but an examination confined to these would not be any test of his literary capacity, of his susceptibility to the poem as a poem.

In these remarks, I assume, of course, that the prime object of a literary examination should be to test not so much a student's knowingness, as his literary capacity, which means a capacity to respond to the spiritual life of a poem, or any other form of literature, in the true sense of the word 'literature.' It is its spiritual life which makes a poem a poem, whatever the thought articulation may be. The student who is capable of such response should rank higher (nobody but a Dr. Dryasdust could deny this) than the student who could answer all questions which the most prolific questioner could ask him, but who could afford no evidence, through his reading of it, that the poem was anything more to him than was a primrose to Wordsworth's 'Peter Bell.'

As the student advances to the higher literature, he should be trained in the higher, more complex vocal functions demanded for its interpretation; he should understand, all along, in his vocal education, the relation of that education to the rendering of works of genius. He should always know what his vocal exercises are for, what relation they have to the interpreting and symbolizing of thought and feeling.

I remember a teacher who advised his scholars--I was one of them--to go out frequently into the open air and exercise their voices. And the poor fellows did go, and 'fright the isle from her propriety' with their bawling without having any conception of what they were bawling for. Their lungs were exercised thereby, but the bawling did nothing for their vocal training.

Vocal exercise must not only be physiologically intelligent, but there must always be some conception back of it which it is the aim of the exercise to realize in the voice. One may have a conception, more or less distinct, of how some very significant sentence in Shakespeare, for example, should be uttered, and yet his voice is not sufficiently obedient to his will and his feelings. He therefore has something to work after, and in time may vocally realize, to his full satisfaction, his conception; and in doing so, he has acquired some new and valuable control of his voice, which he can make use of, whenever required, in the rendering of other expressions.

A true poem is a piece of articulate music which may require to be long practised upon by the voice before all its possible significance and effectiveness be realized. But there must be an ideal back of the practice (merely to keep 'going over' the poem will not do); not, of course, an entirely distinct ideal, it may be more or less vague, but such an ideal as may be got in advance through a responsiveness to its informing life. This ideal will become more and more distinct in the course of the practice.

This is true of every form of art. The artist starts with an ideal more or less vague (but it is an ideal which motives all his work), and this ideal only gradually takes shape in the process of its realization in a picture or a statue. Composing continues to the end. The poet is still composing, still working after a fuller realization of his ideal, when he is making the last verbal change in his poem. (Note 4.) To quote from Browning's 'A Death in the Desert':

God's gift was that man should conceive of truth, And yearn to gain it, catching at mistake As midway help, till he reach fact indeed. The statuary ere he mould a shape Boasts a like gift, the shape's idea, and next The aspiration to produce the same; So, taking clay, he calls his shape thereout, Cries ever, 'Now I have the thing I see': Yet all the while goes changing what was wrought, From falsehood like the truth, to truth itself.

* * * * *

God only makes the live shape at a jet.

Interpretative reading goes on in the same way. After a reader's long familiarity with a poem, and when he thinks he has realized all its possibilities of vocal effectiveness, some new vocal movement on a single word, it may be, is suggested, which is a decided contribution to the effect before reached. The play of Hamlet abounds in little speeches, and single words, even, whose possibilities of expressiveness can hardly be exhausted. Every great poet writes, at times, more significantly than he knows.

In the creation of every great work of genius, a large degree of unconscious might enters; and this unconscious might the reader with the requisite degree of spiritual susceptibility may respond to. This is an activity of the highest order on the part of a reader. Melody, harmony, and every mode of form, are, to some extent, the product of an unconscious might. Deep feeling attracts to itself such elements of language as serve best to conduct it. Assonance, especially, is a manifestation of it. Paradise Lost abounds with the assonance which the dominant feeling of the poet induced.

When Hamlet is subjecting his friends to a searching examination in regard to the appearance of the ghost of his father, he asks 'His beard was grisly?' and then adds, 'no.' (The word is followed by a period, in the Folio.) What a varied expressiveness this little word 'no' admits of! When Macbeth says to his wife, when they are considering the murder of the king, 'If we should fail?' she replies 'We fail?' Though the interrogative is used in the Folio, the period would, perhaps, be the better pointing. However that be, the reading of 'we fail' involves much consideration; and so does the reading of thousands of single words in Shakespeare's Plays.

But, after all, it is not upon inflections and emphases and other vocal functions which pertain more especially to the interpretation of the articulating thought, that the true reader chiefly depends. The most important thing with him is the choral atmosphere in which a spiritualized composition requires to be presented. And it is in this respect that the art of reading particularly corresponds with the sister art of painting. The artist in form and color bathes his landscape in 'the light that never was, on sea or land,' or, if not that, in some light or other, some 'tender light which heaven to gaudy day denies,' and which serves to reveal the feeling which he aimed to express through the landscape. The landscape itself corresponds in painting with the articulating thought in reading; but the spiritual attitude of the artist is exhibited through the light in which the landscape is bathed. And so the spiritual attitude of the reader is exhibited through his intonation, which corresponds with atmosphere in painting. A susceptible reader will, on the first reading of a poem or an impassioned prose composition, be more or less immediately responsive to the key-note of the composition. An increased familiarity will finally bring this key-note fully home to his feelings, or as fully as may be; and if he has made the articulating thought his own, he is now prepared to interpret the composition to the ears of others. A reader's success in interpreting such a poem as Tennyson's In Memoriam, for example, can be but partial if he has not adequately caught, and does not vocally reproduce, the key-note, however distinctly he may present the articulating thought. It is the tone which spiritualizes and quickens the thought; and it is the main object in reading, to spiritualize and quicken thought, to bring it into relation with the spiritual being of the hearer.

Vocal training, the most scientific and systematic, will not of itself make readers, that is, vocal interpreters of genius. Something more must be done than is at present done, in homes and schools, especially in homes, for the education of the spiritual nature; and this education must be begun early, must precede the education of the intellect. The premature forcing open of the bud of reason, which now prevails to a lamentable degree, must receive its due condemnation. It is a thing to be condemned from Christian pulpits. As George Henry Lewes says, in his novel, Ranthorpe, 'the child must feel before it can know; and knowledge, great and glorious as it is, can never be the end of life: it is but one of the many means.'

It is quite superfluous to say that a reader should have a perfect articulation; that he should be able to command a wide range of pitch; all degrees of force, from pianissimo to fortissimo; radical, median, vanishing, and compound stress; every variety of inflection, direct upward and direct downward inflection; equal and unequal, upward and downward, single and double waves; accelerated and retarded utterance; many qualities of voice; not to name numerous other vocal functions and attributes which are means to various kinds of interpretative ends. He should also have a complete knowledge of the language he is rendering, as a living organism,--an indispensable condition of his presenting the successive and involved groups of thought with the requisite distinctness of outline, and with the requisite perspective, determined by their relative value, of which he should have the nicest sense. A very important condition of perspective, I would say by the way, is the light touch which needs to be given to whatever is implied, has been anticipated, should be taken for granted, etc.,--the light touch which conveys the impression that the mind of the reader does not come down upon the parts receiving the same, those parts saying themselves, so to speak, but is occupied with the main current of thought. Any untrained voice can emphasize, but only a trained or a naturally unperverted voice can give the light touch successfully. Yet it is possible for the heaviest, clumsiest voice to be trained to the light touch, to delicacy of tint, just as one who is clay-fisted may, in time, attain to some delicacy of manipulation. The voice and the hand have wonderful possibilities, rarely realized; the former, when converted from the error of its ways, being, indeed, the most expressive organ of the soul; the latter being 'the consummation of all perfection as an instrument.'

One great secret in forcible speech is, that all the force be thrown upon the vowels--the inarticulate elements. While sounding them, the organs of speech are apart, and if the lungs are kept well inflated, the throat is open, and no friction results; while articulating the consonants, certain two of the organs of speech are in contact, and the throat is more or less closed. If force be thrown upon the consonants, the articulate elements, or certain of them, such as r and k, for example, there is more or less friction in the throat. In uttering forcibly the word 'struck,' for example, all the force should be thrown upon the [)u], the consonants str and k being about the same as in ordinary utterance.

The music of speech is chiefly in the vowels. But the consonants must, of course, be distinctly articulated and not be drowned in the vocality.

Sir Henry Taylor writes to Lady Taunton, May 23, 1862 (Correspondence, edited by Edward Dowden), of Tennyson's reading: 'As to his reading, he is a very deep-mouthed hound, and the sound of it is very grand; but I rather need to know by heart what he is reading, for otherwise I find the sense to be lost in sounds from time to time; and, even when I do know what the words are, I think more of articulation is wanted to give the consonantal effects of the rhythm; for without these effects the melodious sinks into the mellifluous in any ordinary utterance; and even when intoned by such an organ as Alfred's, if the poetry be of a high order, the rhythm so sounded loses something of its musical and more of its intellectual significance. In the best verse, not every word only, but every letter, should speak. Nevertheless, his reading is very fine of its kind, and it is a very rare thing to hear fine reading of any kind.'

In regard to inflections, or bends, of the voice, of every kind, direct upward, or downward, or combinations of both, which are called waves (upward waves being a combination of downward and upward inflections, or bends, and downward waves the reverse, and double waves being a combination of upward and downward waves, or the reverse), I would say, what I have said in my 'Primer of English Verse,' that a reader must have a sub-consciousness of a dead level, by which, or from which, to graduate all his departures; and it is only by avoiding all non-significant departures that he imparts to his hearers a sub-consciousness of his own standard. There should never be in reading a non-significant departure from a pure monotony. Significant vocal intervals lose their effectiveness when they are mixed up with non-significant ones. Great effects can be secured through very simple means by a reader who strictly observes this principle. Every little bend of the voice tells. But a wriggling voice, the general tenor of which is a violation of this principle, cannot secure such effects. The hearer is presented with a jumble of non-significant and would-be significant intervals, which is less effective than a pure monotony would be.

Appreciative reading is shown as much, perhaps, in what I will call time melody, as in almost any other feature of vocalization. A reader's sense of the relative values of successive and involved groups of thought, is largely indicated by his varied (melodious) rate of utterance. And much of the pleasure which an appreciative listener derives from reading, as reading, is this indication on the part of the reader of a nice estimate of relative values. He feels that the reader is a qualified interpreter. This estimate cannot always be determined by what a writer makes, syntactically, principal, and what subordinate, in the construction of his language. Of course, a mere variation of time is not, of itself, sufficient. There must be an appropriate variation of tone-color, etc.

A simile or comparison, for example, must be so read as to indicate the reader's estimate of what it illustrates; and this is particularly shown by the accelerated or retarded utterance of it, and by the tone-color given to it.

The following striking simile from II Kings, xxi. 13, should be read with an accelerated utterance, implying the ease with which the act illustrated will be performed: 'And I will stretch over Jerusalem the line of Samaria, and the plummet of the house of Ahab: and I will wipe Jerusalem as a man wipeth a dish, wiping it, and turning it upside down.'

The following comparison (Isaiah, lv. 10, 11) should be read in slower time, in itself considered, and, partly, for the reason that it precedes what it illustrates (a due expectation must be awakened as to what follows): 'As the rain cometh down and the snow from heaven, and returneth not thither, but watereth the earth, and maketh it bring forth and bud, and giveth seed to the sower and bread to the eater; so shall my word be that goeth out of my mouth: it shall not return unto me void, but it shall accomplish that which I please, and it shall prosper in the thing whereto I sent it.'

In still slower time, every appreciative reader would spontaneously read the following comparison (Milton's Paradise Lost, Book I., w. 591-600):

his form had not yet lost All her original brightness; nor appeared Less than archangel ruined, and the excess Of glory obscured: as when the sun, new risen, Looks thro' the horizontal misty air Shorn of his beams; or from behind the moon, In dim eclipse, disastrous twilight sheds On half the nations, and with fear of change Perplexes monarchs. Darken'd so, yet shone Above them all the archangel.

An increased time of utterance must be secured through the prolongable vowels and consonants, rather than through pauses, though the latter must also be somewhat extended. Accelerated utterance must not impress as hurry.

The fifth chapter of the Book of Daniel, descriptive of Belshazzar's feast, affords good illustrations of the slighting of speech. (Note 5.) Take, for example, the first five verses (the parts which should be slighted are indicated by smaller type):

1. Belshazzar, =the king=, made a great feast =to a thousand of his lords=, and drank wine =before the thousand=.

2. Belshazzar, =whiles he tasted the wine=, commanded to bring the golden and silver vessels which his father Nebuchadnezzar had taken out of the temple which was in Jerusalem; =that the king, and his princes, his wives, and his concubines=, might drink therein.

3. =Then they brought the golden vessels that were taken out of the temple of the house of God which was at Jerusalem; and the king and his princes, his wives and his concubines=, drank =in them=.

4. =They drank wine=, and praised the gods of gold, =and of silver, of brass, of iron, of wood, and of stone=.

5. In the same hour came forth fingers =of a man's hand=, and wrote =over against the candlestick upon the plaster of the wall of the king's palace=; and the king saw =the part of the hand that wrote=.

The parts in smaller type have various degrees of subordinate value, which the nicely appreciative reader would indicate by his reading; but they all belong to the background of the description. Any of these parts, if brought fully into the foreground, would be given an undue importance, and would reduce somewhat the prominence and distinctness of the other parts.

In the first verse, 'the king,' should be read with an abatement of voice, being an understood appositive; 'to a thousand of his lords' ('thousand' being used for an indefinite large number), is sufficiently implied in 'gave a great feast,' and the voice should be reduced upon it, and should not descend upon 'lords,' as it is assumed that the feast was given to the chief men of the kingdom; 'and drank wine before the thousand:' the voice after descending upon 'wine,' should drift lightly over 'before the thousand.'

In the second verse, 'whiles he tasted the wine' should, as it were, say itself; and then the command of the king, in regard to the sacred vessels of the temple, should be brought to the front; 'that the king, and his princes, his wives, and his concubines,' should be thrown back with a reduced and somewhat accelerated voice, and prominence given to 'might drink therein,' the purpose being to invite chief attention to the sacrilegious act of making such use of the sacred vessels. A distinct noting of the different kinds of people present at the feast is not called for here. The voice has other business on hand, namely, the bringing forward of the sacrilegious purpose to drink wine from the sacred vessels of the temple. Further on in the chapter, in the speech of Daniel to the king (v. 23), it is necessary to bring these people fully to the front, the melodious movement of the voice being adapted to the special emphasizing of 'thou' and 'concubines,' thus: 'and the, and thy lords, thy wives, and thy concubines,' a somewhat increased pitch and force being given to 'concubines.'

In the third verse, 'Then they brought the golden vessels,' etc., should be read as a matter of course, and not as if it were necessary to invite the attention of the hearer to the fact that the command of the king was obeyed. The latter mode of reading would be wholly gratuitous (as it should be assumed that the command of the king was obeyed), and would waste attention; 'and the king, and his princes, his wives, and his concubines' should be again thrown back, and, the voice should descend somewhat forcibly upon 'drank,' thus marking distinctly the sacrilege.

In the fourth verse, 'They drank wine,' being a mere repetition, should say itself (the mind of the reader not coming down upon it, but keeping along on the upper plane of expression), and the voice should come out strongly upon 'and praised the gods of gold'; but it should be reduced, and somewhat accelerated, upon, 'and of silver, of brass, of iron, of wood, and of stone.' Their idolatry having been sufficiently brought out through 'and praised the gods of gold,' it would waste attention to bring forward also the several other materials of which their gods were composed. These should be expressed, as it were, by the way. The mind of the reader is done with the fact of idolatry.

In the fifth verse, 'In the same hour, came forth fingers ... and wrote,' should be brought fully to the front, an increase of time being given to 'In the same hour,' to mark distinctly the fact that divine vengeance followed close upon the sacrilege of drinking from the sacred vessels of the temple, which was aggravated by their idolatry (the words 'hour,' 'fingers,' and 'wrote,' receiving each the falling inflection); but 'of a man's hand' should be slighted, the voice being kept up on 'hand,' it being assumed that the fingers were, of course, those of a man's hand, or, at least, of a human hand. The place just where the writing was done, 'over against the candlestick upon the plaster of the wall of the king's palace,' being of no special importance, under the circumstances, should be slighted. To bring it to the front would cause an entirely unnecessary expenditure of attention on the part of the hearer. It should be left to its own intrinsic value, without any enforcement from the voice; 'and the king saw' comes to the front, the voice falling upon 'saw,' and drifting down over 'the part of the hand that wrote.'

As additional examples, take the last seven verses of the chapter: they afford illustrations, too, of the marking of the new idea, as distinguished from the important idea, of a sentence considered by itself:

25. And this =is the writing that was written=, MENE, MENE, TEKEL, UPHARSIN.

26. This is the interpretation =of the thing=: MENE; God hath numbered thy kingdom, =and finished it=.

27. TEKEL: =Thou art weighed in the balances, and art= found wanting.

28. PERES: Thy kingdom =is divided, and given to the Medes and Persians=.

29. =Then commanded Belshazzar, and they clothed Daniel with scarlet, and put a chain of gold about his neck, and made a proclamation concerning him, that he should be the third ruler in the kingdom.=

30. In that night was Belshazzar =the king of the Chaldeans slain=.

31. =And Darius the Median= took =the kingdom, being about threescore and two years old=.

In the twenty-fifth verse, 'And this' stands out, 'this' being the new idea, the voice drifting, with some acceleration, over 'is the writing that was written';

'MENE, MENE, TEKEL, UPHARSIN,' that is, 'numbered, numbered, weighed, divisions,' 'mene, mene' being an emphatic repetition. In the twenty-eighth verse, 'peres,' having the same root, and meaning 'divided,' is substituted for 'upharsin.'

In the twenty-sixth verse, 'This is the interpretation' stands out, the voice coming down on 'interpretation' and drifting over, and slighting, 'of the thing.' When 'mene' is pronounced by Daniel, it must be supposed that its meaning is understood, but not its application; the word 'kingdom' must, therefore, be marked with the emphasis; 'and finished it' must be somewhat slighted, as the meaning of the phrase is anticipated in 'numbered.'

In the twenty-seventh verse, the voice moves along with some acceleration, over 'thou art weighed in the balances,' the idea of 'weighed' being anticipated in 'tekel,' and 'art found wanting' is brought strongly out.

In the twenty-eighth verse, 'kingdom' must receive the emphasis, 'divided' being anticipated in 'peres'; 'and given to the Medes and Persians' we must suppose is not altogether new information to Belshazzar, after his having been informed that the division of his kingdom is at hand. He knows who will come into possession of it. This phrase, therefore, must not be brought fully to the front. It must be uttered with some acceleration of the voice and in a way to indicate the supposed feeling of Daniel in regard to the quick work which is to be made of the kingdom.

The twenty-ninth verse should be read with some acceleration of voice, and without any special expression, the reader assuming that the promise made by the king to Daniel, in the sixteenth verse, if he can interpret the writing, was fulfilled. This twenty-ninth verse must not, therefore, be read as imparting new information.

In the thirtieth verse, 'In that night' must be brought fully out, through a time emphasis, to mark how immediate was the fulfilment of Daniel's interpretation; there must be some acceleration of voice upon 'was

Belshazzar the king of the Chaldeans,' and a quite strong emphasis given to 'slain.'

In the thirty-first verse, 'took' is the foreground word, the emphasis of it implying an accordance with Daniel's interpretation; 'being about threescore and two years old,' should be read as a gratuitously affixed fact, having no particular bearing upon what has been related.

Cultivated people cannot away with what is generally understood by 'elocution,' which is rather a vocal and Delsartian display than an honest vocalization, which good reading should be, of what has been intellectually and spiritually assimilated. Reading is not acting. The first thing to be done to bring 'elocution' into good repute (it is certainly not in good repute at present) is to free reading from all strain of expression--to reduce emphasis and attain to the greatest degree of simplicity compatible with the subject-matter. And one important feature of reading which should receive special attention, as a means to this end, is the light touch, which conveys the impression that the mind of the reader does not come down upon the parts receiving the same, those parts expressing what has been anticipated, or should be taken for granted, etc., and constituting the remote background of expression.

The highest result which can be exhibited of literary culture and a corresponding vocal culture, is an organic melody, in the reading of a great poem, the outcome of the poem's organic life. By melody, in reading, is meant that organic variety in the use of all the vocal functions and affections, that arabesqueness of expression, which does not allow the ear of the hearer to detect a regular recurrence of any of these functions and affections. There is melody of pause, of inflection, of rhyme, of rhythm, of time, of force, of emphasis, and of every vocal affection. In truly melodious reading, the design or figure, so to speak, is so arabesque that it is not taken in by the ear of the hearer, and does not come to his consciousness, but it tells effectively on his feelings. And by 'effectively' I specially mean that the feelings are brought into harmony with, into a state of elective attraction for, the contriving creative spirit which moulds the poetic form. Such reading of high poetry is the extreme merit of vocal expression. Some of its principles may be taught; but the vitality of it must be the result of the spiritual education of the reader, must be exhaled spontaneously from his being.

A reader with a nice sense of melody may conceal a deficiency of melody in the poem he is reading; and he may do this, without arbitrarily imposing variety. An imposed variety is not true melody, which must be vital, organic. In the reading of Pope's uniform couplets, for example, he may keep down the rocking-horse movement of the verse (Note 6) by a skilful management of the pauses (which come so uniformly in the middle and at the end of the verses), and of the rhyming words, by an acceleration and retardation of voice wherever these are permissible, by the light touch, and by various other means. To counteract the uniform construction of such verse as the following, for example, from the Essay on Man, without arbitrarily imposing variety, the reader's art must approach the artful:

Warms in the sun, refreshes in the breeze, Glows in the stars, and blossoms in the trees, Lives thro' all life, extends thro' all extent, Spreads undivided, operates unspent; etc. or the following, descriptive of the heroine, in The Rape of the Lock:

On her white breast, a sparkling cross she wore, Which Jews might kiss, and infidels adore. Her lively looks a sprightly mind disclose, Quick as her eyes, and as unfix'd as those: Favors to none, to all she smiles extends; Oft she rejects, but never once offends. Bright as the sun, her eyes the gazers strike, And, like the sun, they shine on all alike. Yet graceful ease, and sweetness void of pride, Might hide her faults, if Belles had faults to hide: If to her share some female errors fall, Look on her face, and you'll forget 'em all.

The absence of enjambement makes it somewhat difficult so to keep down the rhyme emphasis that it may not pester the ear. (Note 7.)

Where a reader's feelings have been melodized by culture, they will protect him against the influence of a too artificial construction of the verse. He will not impose variety, but he will utter humdrum verse, as far as possible, under the conditions of his melodized feeling.

The importance of cultivating the speaking voice is quite as great as that of cultivating the reading voice. Perhaps it is greater; for the speaking voice has a wider and more constant influence--an influence which is exerted in all the relations of life, an influence calming or irritating, an influence bringing men into friendly or unfriendly attitudes toward each other. How demulcent the effect of a gracious voice, and how rasping that of a snappish one! 'The sweetest music,' says Emerson, 'is not in the oratorio, but in the human voice when it speaks from its instant life tones of tenderness, truth, or courage. The oratorio has already lost its relation to the morning, to the sun, and the earth, but that persuading voice is in tune with these.'

Of Emerson's own voice, the Rev. Charles G. Ames, in 'A Memorial Address,' says: 'His speech had a subtle spell,--a charm like Nature's own, so that he affected men like Old Honesty ... so silvery, cheery, sane, fearless!... There was no false ring, no trick to catch applause or to turn off attention from the message to the messenger; no show of knowledge or power or art. One might forget it all next hour, through sheer moral inability to stay at such an unwonted altitude; but while listening to that high discourse it certainly did seem as if we belonged up there,--as if a man ought to make the very earth a pedestal of honor for his feet and wear the sky about his brow as an aureole.'

How much wrath, with its evil consequences, might be averted by soft answers! How much pleasanter an arrival at a hotel might be than it often is, if the slapdash clerk in the office had a voice better attuned to a courteous reception of a guest! or an arrival in New York, from abroad, if a custom-house official knew how to ask, in a civilized way, 'What's in that box?' The question is often asked in a way which has a decidedly indurating effect upon the conscience of a traveller, in regard to dutiable things he may have brought with him. How afflicting the chaotic clatter of high-pitched voices, at a reception, or an evening party! A room jam-full of standing people, 'unaimed prattle flying up and down' (true conversation is out of the question) is hard to endure, even with the prospect of lobster and of chicken salad, ice cream, and numerous other unwholesome things about to be. American girls, before they 'come out,' may talk in a quiet way; but so soon as they 'come out,' many of them think they must show that they have 'come out,' by the high pitch and rapidity of their voices, which quite deprive a nervous man of his self-possession.

How much 'the charm of beauty's powerful glance' may be heightened or lowered by the character of the voice which goes along with it! Woman tells on others by a gracious manner, by the beauty of holiness as it is manifested in all her ways, in all her relations, domestic and social, and especially by her voice. A woman with a sweet and gracious voice, the index of a sweet and gracious nature, may exert through it, in the ordinary relations of life, without even knowing it, a better influence than she could by advisedly devoting herself to doing good, even if such devotion took the form of distributing religious tracts! The moral atmosphere of a home may be not a little due to the voice of the wife and mother. The memory, even, of a voice which was toned by love and sympathy, may continue to be a sweet influence long after the voice itself has been hushed in death. The influence of the voice for good or evil, in the domestic, social, and all other relations of life, cannot be estimated. A voice may even have a good or bad reflex action upon its possessor. A slovenly articulation, for example, may be the index of a moral slovenliness, and may react upon the latter. Subtle, indeed, and imperceptible, are the influences upon ourselves, for good or evil, of all our commonest doings.

A fond, worldly mother may be anxiously ambitious that her daughter shall have all the accomplishments required for her fullest attractiveness when she 'comes out.' Years may be spent upon her musical education, with the poor result, perhaps, of 'fine sleights of hand and unimagined fingering, shuffling off the hearer's soul through hurricanes of notes to a noisy Tophet'; she may be taught dancing which rivals that of a Taglioni, and French, and drawing, and painting; she may be sent abroad to snatch the graces beyond the reach of art, of the most elegant European society; and yet, in the grand scheme of accomplishments, the speaking voice is left out and entirely neglected, though she have a voice unpleasantly pitched, and with other remediable defects which are far, very far, from idealizing, transfiguring her! If the time devoted to the piano, with the supposed poor result, had been devoted to a careful cultivation of her voice, her power to charm (that being the end proposed) would be much more increased than by any or all of her other accomplishments.

It is easy to infer what Shakespeare's opinions were on many subjects, although his Plays are regarded by some critics as peculiarly impersonal; but they are charged with his personality, and shadow forth, not dimly, his views in regard to many things. The evidence is abundant that the voice was to him very significant, apart from his estimate of its importance, as a professional actor, and that he was most susceptible to its charms and to its defects. It is her voice which the grief-stricken Lear is made to speak of, when he bends over the dead Cordelia: 'Her voice,' he says, 'was ever soft, gentle, and low'; and to this he adds, 'an excellent thing in woman'; Shakespeare, no doubt, meaning that he had in his mind, at the time, the cruel voices, expressive of their hard and wicked hearts, of Regan and Goneril. After the death of Antony, Cleopatra, in her rapturous praise of him, says,---

His voice was propertied As all the tuned spheres, and that to friends; But when he meant to quail and shake the orb, It was as rattling thunder.

Hamlet's advice to the players we may take as an expression of Shakespeare's own standard of vocal delivery, and as his protest against a stilted and ranting declamation, which, no doubt, characterized many of the actors of his day.

There is evidence in the Plays that, in the process of composition, he must either have heard imaginatively what he was writing, or have actually voiced his language as he went along. He did not write for the eye, but for the ear. And the high vocal capabilities of his language may be somewhat attributable to his hearing of what he wrote. Must he not have heard the effect of monosyllabic words, uttered with the tremor and semi-tone of old age, when he wrote King Lear's speeches?--'You see me here, you gods, a poor old man, as full of grief as age,' etc., and 'When we are born, we cry that we are come to this great stage of fools,' etc. And must he not have heard the effect of polysyllabic words as expressive of Macbeth's sense of the vastness of his guilt, when he wrote, 'this my hand will rather the multitudinous seas incarnadine,' etc.? of the guttural emphasis, expressive of detestation, in the speech of Coriolanus to the rabble?--'You common cry of curs! whose breath I hate as reek o' the rotten fens,' etc.

An interesting compilation might be made from the Plays, of passages expressive of strong passion of various kinds, the several vocabularies of which testify to Shakespeare's having imaginatively or actually voiced what he wrote. The speech of the Bastard to Hubert, in King John (A. iv. S. 3), is a signal example:

Bastard. Here's a good world!--Knew you of this fair work? Beyond the infinite and boundless reach Of mercy, if thou didst this deed of death, Art thou damn'd, Hubert.

Hubert. Do but hear me, sir.

Bastard. Ha! I'll tell thee what; Thou'rt damn'd as black--nay, nothing is so black; Thou art more deep damn'd than Prince Lucifer: There is not yet so ugly a fiend of hell As thou shalt be, if thou didst kill this child.

I fancy that Shakespeare had a fine voice. If he had not, it is quite certain that he had the highest estimate and appreciation of the voice as the organ of the soul. His creative spirit, too, attracted to itself the most effective vocabulary for the vocal expression of every kind of passion--the most effective by reason of their monosyllabic or their polysyllabic character, of their vowel or their consonantal elements. To him, language was for the ear, not for the eye. The written word was to him what it was to Socrates, 'the mere image or phantom of the living and animated word.' (Note 8.)

The art of printing has caused language to be overmuch transferred from its true domain, the sense of hearing, to the sense of sight. The lofty idealized language of poetry is known, in these days, chiefly through the eye, and its true power is consequently quiescent for the generality of silent readers. In silent reading, an appreciation of matter and form must be largely due to an imaginative transference to the ear of what is taken in by the eye.

The impression seems to be getting stronger and stronger, in these days of excessive teaching and excessive learning, that no one can do anything or learn anything without being taught,--without 'taking a regular course,' as the phrase is. This seems to be especially true in the matter of vocal cultivation. People go to schools of oratory with nothing within themselves which is clamorous for expression; not even a very 'still small voice' urging them to express something. Many who desire, or think they do, to be readers, as there are many who desire, or think they do, to be artists, evidently believe that if they be trained in technique they can be readers or artists.

But suppose some one is impelled to cultivate vocal power because of his desire to express what he has sympathetically and lovingly assimilated, of a work of genius: if he endeavor to give an honest expression, so far as in him lies, to what he feels, and avoid trying to express what he does not feel, and if he persevere in his endeavor, with always a coefficient ideal back of his reading, he may--in time, he certainly will--become a better reader than another could if he should set out, with malice prepense, to be an elocutionist, and with that malicious purpose, were to employ a mere voice-trainer who should teach him to perpetrate all sorts of vocal extravagances, to make faces, and to gesticulate when reading what does not need any gesture. Such an one, after passing out of the hands of his trainer, is most likely to go forth and afflict the public with his performances, which will be wholly a pitiable exhibition of himself.

Some of the best readers I have ever known have been of the former class, who honestly voiced what they had sympathetically assimilated, and did not strain after effect. But it seems that when one sets out to read, with no interior capital, he or she, especially she, is apt to run into all kinds of extravagances which disgust people of culture and taste. The voice, instead of being the organ of the soul, is the betrayer of soullessness.

Without that interior life which can respond to the indefinite life of a work of genius (indefinite, that is, to the intellect), a trained voice can do nothing of itself in the way of real interpretation. It may bring out the definite articulating thought, in a way, but the electric aura in which the thought should be enveloped, will be wanting; and where this is wanting, in the expression of spiritualized thought, the true object of reading is but imperfectly realized. What can be got through the eye, it is not the main function of the voice to deliver. There must be the requisite 'drift' and choral intonation--drift, the air, the pervading, ruling spirit, 'the dominant's persistence,' the prevailing tone color.

I am pleased to quote, in this connection, what Professor Edward Dowden writes in his article on 'The teaching of English literature,' contained in his recent volume, 'New Studies in Literature': 'Few persons nowadays seem to feel how powerful an instrument of culture may be found in modest, intelligent, and sympathetic reading aloud. The reciter and the elocutionist of late have done much to rob us of this which is one of the finest of the fine arts. A mongrel something which, at least with the inferior adepts, is neither good reading nor yet veritable acting, but which sets agape the half-educated with the wonder of its airs and attitudinizing, its pseudo-heroics and pseudo-pathos, has usurped the place of the true art of reading aloud, and has made the word "recitation" a terror to quiet folk who are content with intelligence and refinement. Happily in their behalf the great sense-carrier to the Empire, Mr. Punch, has at length seen it right to intervene. (Note 9.) The reading which we should desire to cultivate is intelligent reading, that is, it should express the meaning of each passage clearly; sympathetic reading, that is, it should convey the feeling delicately; musical reading, that is, it should move in accord with the melody and harmony of what is read, be it in verse or prose.'

A training of the organs of speech which brings them into complete obedience to the will and the feelings, and a perfect technique, important and indispensable as they are, cannot, of themselves, avail much in the interpretation of spiritualized thought. This must be mainly the result of such education as induces an inward preparedness for responding to and assimilating the essential life of a work of genius. Quicquid recipitur, recipitur ad modum recipientis (whatever is received, is received according to the measure of the recipient). And it is, or should be, the leading object of literary education to enlarge the spiritual measure of the recipient.

Now it must be said that the schools, with all their grammars, their rhetorics, their philologies, their psychologies, their histories and cheap philosophies of literature, their commentaries and annotations, do not prepare their students to know works of genius in their absolute character; for such knowledge implies an adequate education of the absolute, that is, spiritual man, and such education is not induced by the above studies as at present conducted. It demands spiritual life to respond to spiritual life; or, in the words of St. Paul, 'the natural man receiveth not the things of the Spirit of God, for they are foolishness unto him; neither can he know them, because they are spiritually discerned.'

What is generally understood in the schools as a thorough study of a work of genius, is occupied quite exclusively with the language and with that part of the subject-matter which can be intellectually formulated. That part which demands a spiritual response and which it is the main object of reading to vocalize for the purpose of calling forth such response, is not included in the so-called thorough study. The latter may do much, indeed, to shut off any spiritual response which a student might give if he were not subjected to such study. In this statement no depreciation of scholarship is meant to be implied. Let us have the most thorough scholarship possible; but it must not become an end to itself; it must be a means to the higher end of intellectual and spiritual life.

What chiefly afflicts a cultivated hearer, in 'elocution,' is the conspicuous absence of spiritual assimilation on the part of the reader. At best, he voices only what the eye of an ordinary reader could take in, and leaves the all-important part to his face, arms, and legs, and various attitudes of the body. But the spiritual in literature must be addressed to the ear. 'A spirit aerial informs the cell of Hearing,' says Wordsworth, in his great poem, 'On the power of sound.'

Reading, I have said, is not acting. It is the acting which usually accompanies the reading or recitation of the professional elocutionist which cultivated people especially dislike. When they wish to see acting, they prefer going to a theatre. When they listen to reading, they want serious interpretative vocalization; only that and nothing more is necessary, unless it be a spontaneous and graceful movement of the hands, occasionally, such as one makes in animated conversation.

Again, the most elegant way of vocally interpreting a poem, is to read it from a book, rather than to recite it. Recitation has much to do with this acting business. In fact, elocutionists recite in order to have their arms free to act--to illustrate the thought they are expressing. Thought should not be helped out by gesture. Gesture results, or should result, from emotion, and should, therefore, be indefinite. Mimetic gesture, or mimetic action of any kind, is rarely, if ever, in place. If a speaker, addressing a very ignorant audience, had to use the word 'rotatory,' for example, he might make a cyclic movement or two with his hand, to illustrate its meaning. But to do so before an audience presumably intelligent enough to know the meaning of the word, would be impertinent--a 'wasteful and ridiculous excess.' So, too, it would be, to illustrate the word 'somersault,' before an audience of ordinary intelligence. The absurdity of mimetic action is well illustrated in the following: 'I have heard,' says a writer in 'Expression' (Vol. I., No. 2), published in Boston, 'of a popular public reader of Boston giving last season Wordsworth's "Daffodils"; and as she came to the last two lines,--

And then my heart with pleasure fills, And dances with the daffodils,

she put her hand to her heart and with pleasure indicated by a sentimental flash of the eye upon the audience, danced a few graceful steps expressive of exuberant joy, and bowed herself off the platform amid the vociferous applause of the audience. The reader's taste in this case was no worse than that of the audience that applauded her. The incident shows how great the general lack of taste, and the need of the systematic study of fitness in the relation of thought to its expression.'

I would say rather than 'lack of taste,' lack of spiritual life, although the former is closely allied with the latter. A reader who has assimilated the 'Daffodils,' who can sympathetically reproduce within himself the heart-dance of the poet, can better reveal that reproduction through the voice (the requisite vocal culture being assumed) than through such mimetic foolery as the above. He would not and could not condescend to the latter, if he had feeling deep enough truly to know the poem of the 'Daffodils.' True feeling is always serious, even if it be that of deep joy. The trouble with many public readers is, that they don't truly know, have not inwardly experienced, what they attempt to interpret vocally; and, as a consequence, they resort to what disgusts people of real culture.

I was once present, by accident, at a lecture given by a Delsarto-elocutionary woman, and in the course of the lecture, she presented what, she said, would be false gestures in reciting Whittier's Maud Muller. She then recited the poem, with, according to her notions, true gestures, which were more in number than Cicero made, perhaps, in his orations against Cataline, or Demosthenes, in his oration On the Crown. Every idea of the poem told outwardly on her body.

If a woman, in reading Maud Muller, has emotions which must find vent in gesture, and various physical contortions, she ought to be put under treatment that would tone up her system.

The University of the Future, in order to be a vastly greater power than the University of the Present, must, at least, rank spiritual education with intellectual training and discipline. This the University of the near Future must do; the University of a more remote Future, we must believe, if we believe that the spiritual is the crowning attribute of man--that by which he is linked with the permanent, the eternal, will make all intellectual training and discipline, even all physical training, so far as may be, subservient to the spiritual man.

Let us cry 'All good things Are ours, nor soul helps flesh more, now, than flesh helps soul!'

The rectification of the intellect must, as the greatest poem of the century, Browning's 'Ring and the Book,' implicitly teaches, be through the rectification of the spiritual, absolute man.

As bearing directly on my leading subject, the vocal interpretation of literature (that is, spiritualized thought), I would indicate some of the means and conditions of a more spiritual education than is contemplated in the most advanced educational schemes of the day.

What may be said to be the predominant idea of the present day, entertained especially by scientists and exercising its influence, more or less, on the great majority of minds, in regard to the main avenue to knowledge and truth? I answer, and I think not unjustifiably, the idea that the analytic, discursive, generalizing intellect, is adequate to solve all solvable problems-- that it is the only reliable means of arriving at a positive knowledge; that, accordingly, education, the highest education, consists almost exclusively in learning and in being trained to discover and apply, the laws, so called, of nature, to trace facts to their (scientific) causes and to advance logically from causes to facts--that upon which the analyzing and generalizing intellect cannot be exercised, being set down as unknowable. Of an intuition inaccessible to analysis, they take little or no account. This some future age, with a more complete education, than ours, will, I am persuaded, regard as the cardinal defect in the education and philosophy of the present age--a defect that tends to deaden, if not to destroy, in many minds, all faith in those spiritual instincts and spiritual susceptibilities and apprehensions, which constitute the basis of a living hope and faith in immortality, and through which, and through which alone, man may know, without thought, some of the highest truths, truths which are beyond the reach of the discourse of reason. While the reasoning faculties of a man may exist in vigor, the ties which unite the soul sympathetically and through assimilation, with universal spirituality, may be sundered, and a spiritual world for him there will then be none.

That there are higher and subtler organs of discernment than the discursive intellect, and higher things to be discerned than can be discerned by the senses, the lowliest of men and women, no less than the most exalted in intellect and genius, have, throughout the whole recorded history of the race, borne an incontrovertible testimony. 'The natural condition of humanity,' says William Howitt, 'is alliance with the spiritual; the anti-spiritual is but an epidemic--a disease.'

Great have been the conquests of Science, the last fifty years, and great has been their influence on the temporal well-being of mankind. But it must be admitted, perhaps, that these conquests, the product mainly of the insulated intellect, have been somewhat at the expense of 'the interior divinity.'

Wordsworth, addressing his friend Coleridge, in the second book of 'The Prelude,' says: to thee Science appears but what in truth she is, Not as our glory and our absolute boast, But as a succedaneum, and a prop To our infirmity. He has been speaking of mental science.

The present signs of the times, however, give promise that humanity, far as it has drifted in one direction, will assert its wholeness, and will 'render unto Caesar the things that are Caesar's, and unto God the things that are God's,' and that the awakening of 'the interior divinity,' of the spiritual instincts and intuitions, will be as much the aim of the education of the future as the exercise of the mere intellect now is. This awakening must begin in infancy, when the child first 'rounds to a separate mind,' and can respond to its mother's smile, and feel her protecting care, and the rosy warmth of her love. Then will the wise mother regard her child as almost wholly an impressionable being, and will see especially to its surroundings and its associations whether they are suitable to be stamped upon its plastic mind. As it grows, she will aim to quicken and purify it sentiment, and to cultivate a love of the beautiful in form, in color, in sound, especially as these are exhibited in the works of Nature; will endeavor to bring it into the fullest sympathy with all forms of animal life, down to 'the meanest thing that feels.' It is a good sign when a boy loves animals and is kind to them; but when he is bent on killing things, it can be quite safely inferred that he has not received at home lessons in love and had his sympathies and affections duly awakened. Home-life in this country is not, as a general thing, such as to bring the best affections into a healthy play. There is too much worry, too much taking thought of the morrow, too much dissatisfaction with the present condition, too much eagerness to get rich. Some fathers never sufficiently dismiss their business and cares from their minds, to play with their children and to show them those little attentions which their young hearts crave; and mothers expend their souls in the cares and vexations of housekeeping, or, if, by reason of their position and wealth, they are free from these, in social or other matters which shut them off, more or less, from those maternal functions which they should consider it their highest duty to exercise. Filial affection certainly does not increase in this country, as the years go on. Is it too much to say, perhaps it is, that it is rather the exception than the rule, for children, after, and often before, their majority, to show a strong attachment either for their parents or for each other? And there is a word in our language that has quite survived its usefulness; and if things continue to go on as they are now going, it will soon be a fit subject for an Archaic Dictionary--I mean the word REVERENCE. It still maintains its place in our Dictionaries of living vocables, but the thing it represents is a rara avis in terris nigroque simillima cygno. Vain is the attempt to awaken the religious sentiment in a child, to cause it to feel the real significance of the words, as it utters them, 'Our

Father who art in heaven,' in whom the filial and the reverential sentiments are quite extinguished. These sentiments are the soil in which the religious sentiment can best germinate, grow, bud, and fragrantly bloom.

During a child's earliest years the foundation should be laid for that spiritual relationship with Nature which Wordsworth has presented in his great autobiographic poem, 'The Prelude.' Such relationship but very few could realize in themselves as the great high priest of Nature realized it; but all could be brought into a more intimate spiritual relationship with Nature than is favored and promoted, at present, by home influences and by school studies. The latter, when prematurely analytical, and brain slaughtering, tend rather to shut off such relationship.

What is understood as a scientific observation of nature, is not its highest form, so far, at least, as spiritual culture is concerned. It is almost exclusively an analytic observation, in which the conscious intellect plays the chief part. It is study, not spiritual communion. The highest form of observation (if observation it can strictly be called, which is to so great an extent a rapture of necessity and spontaneity) is that which results from the synthetic play of the spiritual faculties, and brings the outer world and all its minutest features into relation with the inner world of man's spirit, and makes him feel his great allies. It is this kind of observation rather than the other, which 'adds a precious seeing to the eye,' and gives to a man some measure of 'the vision and the faculty divine,' and enables him to know something of the fields that are his own; but from which spiritual torpor may alienate him.

'I, long before the blissful hour arrives,' writes Wordsworth, meaning when the discerning intellect of man shall be wedded to this goodly universe in love and holy passion, and shall find the ideal forms of Poets, a simple produce of the common day,

I, long before the blissful hour arrives, Would chant, in lonely peace, the spousal verse Of this great consummation;--and, by words Which speak of nothing more than what we are, that is, what we really or potentially are,

Would I arouse the sensual from their sleep Of death, and win the vacant and the vain To noble raptures; while my voice proclaims How exquisitely the individual mind (And the progressive powers perhaps no less Of the whole species) to the external World Is fitted:--and how exquisitely, too-- Theme this but little heard of among men-- The external world is fitted to the mind; etc.

The system of general spiritual education which is both explicitly and implicitly set forth in 'The Prelude,' makes this great autobiographical poem one of the most valuable productions in English Literature; and teachers capable of bringing its informing spirit home to their students (capable by virtue of their own assimilation of it), might do great things in the way of a spiritual quickening of their students.

And how much capable mothers might derive from Wordsworth's poetry for the spiritual nurture of their children! Capable mothers are, alas! comparatively few; but forces, to be noticed further on, are now at work, which are increasing the number of such mothers, and will continue to increase it more and more, as the ideals of a true womanhood are more and more exalted and realized. The kind of regeneration which the world, at present, most needs, will have to be largely induced by woman, and she will induce it according as her true rights, which are involved in her 'distinctive womanhood,' are recognized and granted her, by her not over-generous brother.

Spiritual education is not a matter of abstract instruction. It must be induced on the basis of the concrete and the personal. The spiritual faculties have no affinities for the abstract. Christianity was introduced into the world through the personal and concrete; rather, it is the personal and the concrete, and its arch-enemy has ever been the abstract, in the form of dogma and stark-naked doctrine. Dogmatism implies materialism. As one advances spiritually, dogma declines with him, in inverse proportion. Christianity is essential being, and not a doctrine, not a body of opinions, not 'a matter of antiquarian pedantry or of historical perspective.' In the great words of the 'De Imitatione Christi,' 'Cui ernum verbum loquitur, ille a multis opinionibus expeditur' (he to whom the eternal word speaks, is freed from many opinions); and to fit the soul to be spoken to by the eternal word, is the true, the ultimate object of spiritual education. The permanent, the eternal, that which is alive for evermore, should, indeed, be the object of all education. Phenomena, in themselves, are not educative. A feeding on them alone, if that were possible (man naturally, whatever his condition, seeks other pabulum), would soon result in a general atrophy of all the faculties, intellectual and spiritual. To use the words of St. Vincent de Lins, which he applied to the Catholic Church,-- would that the Church had always made them its controlling principle!-- 'magnopere curandum est ut id teneamus quod ubique, quod semper, quod ab omnibus creditum est' (it must be especially seen to, that we hold to that which everywhere, which always, which by all, has been believed).

There is no exclusiveness in the eternal word; it speaks to every one whose ears are open to it; it enters wherever it is not shut out. It speaks through Nature, through every form of Art (which to be art must be a manifestation of it), through Poetry, 'the breath and finer spirit of all knowledge,' through Music, Sculpture, Painting, Architecture, through all sacred books, and, above all, through sanctified men and women, of the Present and the Past, 'the noble Living and the noble Dead.' In the words of Emerson:

Not from a vain or shallow thought His awful Jove young Phidias brought; Never from lips of cunning fell The thrilling Delphic oracle; Out from the heart of nature rolled The burdens of the Bible old; The litanies of nations came, Like the volcano's tongue of flame, Up from the burning core below,-- The canticles of love and woe.

* * * * *

The word unto the prophet spoken Was writ on tables yet unbroken; The word by seers or sibyls told In groves of oak or fanes of gold Still floats upon the morning wind, Still whispers to the willing mind.

The kind of books which the young should read, is, of course, an important consideration. If 'a general insight into useful facts' be regarded as the main thing in a child's education, such as 'the royal genealogies of Oviedo, the internal laws of the Burmese empire, by how many feet Mount Chimborazo outsoars Teneriffe, what navigable river joins itself to Lara, and what census of the year five was taken at Klagenfurt,' and other matters not having much to do with the advancement of the millennium, why the question is easily settled as to the kind of books a child should be provided with, and be required to learn, and recite; but if some vitality of soul, the indispensable condition of intellectual vitality, in after life, be the aim, then a different kind of books will be needed--such books as will serve to vitalize and guide the instincts, to bring the feelings into a healthful play, and awaken enthusiasm, and thus to prepare the way for the later exercise of the reasoning faculties, and for the comprehension of moral and religious principles. There is a time to feel the True, the Beautiful, and the Good, and a time to regard all these, as far as may be, under intellectual relations. If 'the years that bring the philosophic mind' be anticipated in a child's education, it will be likely, by reason of the premature philosophy served out to it, to become a stupid man or woman, with a plentiful lack of both intellect and soul. Upon the closed bud of reason, while it is not yet ready to be unfolded, must be brought to bear the genial warmth of sensibility, sympathy, and enthusiasm; and when it opens in its own good season, it will not be dwarfed nor canker-bitten.

Sensibility, sympathy, enthusiasm, I repeat, are the elements of the atmosphere in which the intellectual, the moral, and the religious nature of a child can alone germinate and healthily grow, and in later years, bloom and shed a wholesome fragrance.

Stories written for the young must be concrete representations of the True, the Beautiful, and the Good; in other words, they must be works of art. Says Browning, in 'The Ring and the Book,' Art may tell a truth Obliquely, do the thing shall breed the thought, that is, bring what is implicit within the soul, into the right attitude to become explicit--bring about a silent adjustment through sympathy induced by the concrete (it cannot be induced by the abstract); in other words, prepare the way for the apprehension of the truth--do the thing shall breed the thought, Nor wrong the thought, missing the mediate word; that is, Art, so to speak, is the word made flesh,--is the truth, and, as Art, has nothing directly to do with an explicit presentation of the truth. 'The highest, the only operation of Art, as of Nature,' says Goethe, 'is formation' (Gestaltung).

So may you paint your picture, twice show truth, Beyond mere imagery on the wall,-- So, note by note, bring music from your mind, Deeper than ever the Andante dived,-- So write a book shall mean, beyond the facts, Suffice the eye and save the soul beside.

The greatest moral teachers the world has ever known, have exhibited the least of explicit moralizing. They have embodied their gospels,--clothed them in circumstance,--woven them into a tissue of imagery and incident and, by so doing, have given them that vitality which alone can awaken sympathy, and thus induce a mental preparedness for a reception of the higher truths, and a comprehension of great principles. A deep sympathy with truth is the important thing: this implies a rectification of the spiritual nature--its harmonization with the constitution of things. A great amount of abstract truth may be lodged in one's brain, and this sympathy may be more or less wanting. To secure it, the 'Word' of the teacher must become flesh,--it must be contemplated in the flesh, living and breathing,--it must be represented as militant, subject to accident and antagonism, but assuring men of its unquenchable vitality, its relationship with the divine, through the might of its resistance, and through its final triumph, though not necessarily according to earthly standards of the triumphant. There are novels which exhibit a somewhat low ideal of life through the general squaring up of things at the end--the good being rewarded outwardly and the bad punished. But

In the corrupted 'currents of this world, Offence's gilded hand may shove by justice, ... but 'tis not so above.

The teachings of Jesus are clothed in circumstance and imagery which were familiar to all whom he addressed. 'All these things spake Jesus unto the multitude in parables; and without a parable spake he not unto them.' To use the words of Archbishop Trench in his 'Unconscious Prophecies of Heathendom,' 'In his life and person, the idea and the fact at length kissed each other, and were thenceforward wedded forever.'

The liberal-minded reader of the four records which we have of Christ's life and teachings, must admit that he added little or nothing to the previously existing knowledge of truth in the abstract; he rather caused truth which philosophers and moralists had already intellectually recognized, to be known 'by heart.' He presented it concretely, in his own life and in his teachings, and thus worked it into that 'daily bread' for which he commanded us to pray, and which alone will nourish human sympathy and love. In its previous intellectual, abstract form, it did not, and could not, become an element of spiritual life.

In the thirty beautiful little stories in the New Testament, educators of the young, and indeed all educators in the fullest sense, may see the cardinal principle of their calling, namely, that the greatest power of ethical and religious truth can be secured only through the concrete, and the personal, through that which is the truth, and not through an abstract enunciation-- through that form which is loved for its own sake; whose beauty is its own excuse for being; and the sense of love and beauty, when awakened, makes all things plain. Ubi caritas, ibi claritas.

Many who have written books for the young professedly to impart Christian instruction, have least observed the mode exhibited in the teachings of him whom they profess to take as their Great Exemplar. Their instruction is too explicit. It is presented without a sufficiency of concrete clothing to keep it warm; sometimes in its abstract nakedness. It is thus powerless to awaken the love and sympathy of young hearts.

If the views above expressed are sound, I would say that, in choosing reading matter for the young, special preference should be given to such stories as serve to awaken the imagination, exercise the sympathies, and nourish a lively and joyous enthusiasm. I should wholly exclude explicitly moral and religious stories, and should choose in their stead, stories of human sympathy and sacrifice, heroic endurance, and unconscious virtues (conscious virtue is always weak), fairy tales, and legends gay and sad. A child of healthful, unperverted feelings is averse to moral and religious books, as a class. It would rather read about Robinson Crusoe and his faithful man Friday, and it is far better that it should have such preference--far better that it should live, while a child, in the golden prime Of good Haroun Alraschid, instead of being prematurely crammed with, to it, lifeless moral and religious principles, 'useful' knowledge, and the sciences. Wholesome to every one would be such 'Recollections of the Arabian Nights' as are expressed by Tennyson:

'Far off, and where the lemon-grove In closest coverture upsprung, The living airs of middle night Died round the bulbul as he sung; Not he: but something which possessed The darkness of the world, delight, Life, anguish, death, immortal love, Ceasing not, mingled, unrepressed, Apart from place, withholding time, But flattering the golden prime Of good Haroun Alraschid.'

A child cannot be made virtuous by maxims. The life which is before it, is not a scheme to be taught, but a drama to be acted.

Who loves not Knowledge? Who shall rail Against her beauty? May she mix With men and prosper! Who shall fix Her pillars? Let her work prevail.

But

What is she, cut from love and faith, But some wild Pallas from the brain Of Demons? Let her know her place; She is the second, not the first. Man must grow not alone in power And knowledge, but by year and hour In reverence and in charity.

Blessings upon all the books that are the delight of childhood and youth and unperverted manhood! Precious are the sympathetic tears which dim the page and which it is so wholesome to encourage in early life as a check to the growth of selfishness and egoism. 'Who,' writes George Sand, in her 'Lettres d'un Voyageur,' 'does not remember with delight, the first books which he relished and devoured? Has never an old dusty cover of some volume found upon the shelves of a neglected closet, brought back to your mind the lovely pictures of early years? Are you not again, in fancy, seated in the green meadow bathed in the evening sunlight, where you read it for the first time?'

What galleries of sweet, pathetic, inspiriting, and noble pictures, have been prepared for the modern child!--pictures, which time and all the damp and cold of after life cannot obscure, to those who have enjoyed them. And to what a goodly company is it the privilege of childhood and youth, and early manhood, to be admitted!--the immortal offspring of cheerful genius, whose companionship expands and strengthens and purifies the heart.

But the young are lamentably debarred, in these days of excessive, and non-educating, learning, from the wholesome influences, wholesome, in the way of inducing sympathy, enthusiasm, and a play of the imagination, which the best books of the past and of the present might exert upon them. Their school tasks and examinations absorb all their time, and the accompanying worry about 'marks,' saps their minds--'Death loves a shining mark.'

Later on, in the higher schools, colleges, and universities, there is no time for communion with great authors. The reading which is done, is largely perfunctory. Speaking from my own long experience, I do not think that one out of twenty of university students, even of those who elect courses in English Literature, has read and assimilated the works of any one good author, or any single work. This is a statement based on an exceptionally long experience. Many have studied literature, as the phrase goes, but have no literary education, however well they may have 'passed' in the kind of work done. And such students pursue the study of elocution, with a sufficiently pitiable result. They have never had awakened in them the faculties which are demanded for assimilating the life of a work of genius, and consequently can do nothing in the way of vocal interpretation. They cannot give through the voice, however well trained it may be, what is not theirs to give.

Believing as I do, in the imperative need of the kind of education I have suggested, I must, as a natural consequence, believe in the co-education of the sexes, in the opening to women of all the avenues along which men only have hitherto gone, and in the removal of all obstacles to the exercise of the powers inherent in 'distinctive womanhood.' These things will do more for civilization, in the highest sense of the word, that is, the spiritual sense, than all other agencies combined. A true manhood and a true womanhood cannot be reached except through the mutual influence of the sexes upon each other. They must be educated together, such education beginning in the family, and continuing through all stages of scholastic training up to and through the university. Boys at home, without affectionate sisters, and girls without affectionate brothers, are at a disadvantage. At no less disadvantage is either sex when separated from the other, in school, college, or university. For it is only at this period of their lives, and in such relations, that they can be fitted, if fitted at all, to walk the world together, yoked in all exercise of noble end.

The moral insight of man, to say nothing of his finer spiritual insight, owes much of its penetrating clearness to the feminine element of his nature; and unless this element be developed in due proportion to the intellectual element, he can have, at best, but distorted views of right and wrong, justice and injustice. On this side of his nature, the rays of an unclouded womanhood must strike, before it can be awakened into a genial vitality, and thus impart health, vigor, and subtlety to the intellectual side. 'You cannot think,' says Ruskin (Sesame and Lilies: 2. Of Queen's Gardens), 'that the buckling on of the knight's armor by his lady's hand was a mere caprice of romantic fashion. It is the type of an eternal truth--that the soul's armor is never well set to the heart unless a woman's hand has braced it; and it is only when she braces it loosely that the honor of manhood fails.' On the other hand, woman can be a true woman, only to the degree to which she is permitted to share with man all his highest interests, to sympathize with all his noblest aims, and to work side by side with him in the regeneration of the world. That which is especially distinctive in her nature, must be subdued, toned, and guided by a greater breadth and solidity of intellectual culture; and this can be most effectually secured by co-education, and by her being afforded the opportunity to move with man along the higher planes of learning and of thought, and to have a larger share with him than she has hitherto had, in the fruits of the world's intellectual and moral conquests.

The general recognition and realization which are near at hand, of woman's equal rights with man in all that pertains to the highest good of a human being, will have an especially beneficial influence in the marriage relation, the most important in its bearings of all the relations of human life. There are numberless husbands who pass in society for kind and generous men, recognizing the rights of all with whom they have dealings, and cheerfully according those rights, but who are, in many ways, ungenerous and inconsiderate toward their wives, and that, too, without being in the least aware of it. They would be very much surprised if any one were to tell them so. And why is this? It is, no doubt, in most cases, because of a feeling engendered by the whole past constitution of society--a feeling that has become so ingrained as to be an unconscious one--that woman has peculiar duties which she must fulfil, but that her rights, apart from these peculiar duties, depend upon the arbitrary will of man. Children, from a very early age, are made to feel this more or less, according to the influences of their home-life. When a father shows no estimate of the mother's opinions and advice, never talks with her on the higher current subjects of interest, nor consults her about the weightier matters with which he has to deal, but regards her (and this he may do in all kindness) as one whose sole business it is to look well to the ways of her household, the son's ideal of woman is not likely to be the highest. Happy indeed is he whose home education has been such that 'faith in womankind beats with his blood.' That, by itself, is a liberal education.

Fears are entertained by many good people, that co-education, and woman's larger co-operation with man in the affairs of the world, will tend to unsex her, to render her mannish, and eclipse, more or less, those qualities and graces which have hitherto been regarded as constituting the chief charm and glory of her sex. She may, indeed, have less of mere femineity, but, in its stead, she will certainly have more womanliness, in the best sense of the word (by virtue of which she is a specially commissioned regenerating power in the world), if she is reared and educated with the other sex, and allowed her full share in all the great interests of human life, social, political, educational, moral, and religious. Under such circumstances she has a better chance of becoming

A perfect Woman, nobly planned, To warn, to comfort, and command, than if she be excluded from those interests and lead the restricted life she has ever been obliged to lead by the conventionalities and regulations of society.

The great Italian patriot, Giuseppe Mazzini, 'the prophet and spiritual hero of his nation,' and, indeed, of the whole modern world, wrote in 1858: 'Seek in woman not merely a comfort, but a force, an inspiration, the redoubling of your intellectual and moral faculties. Cancel from your mind every idea of superiority over her. You have none whatever.

'Long prejudice, an inferior education, and a perennial legal inequality and injustice have created that apparent intellectual inferiority which has been converted into an argument of continued oppression.... Like two distinct branches springing from the same trunk, man and woman are varieties springing from the common basis--Humanity. There is no inequality between them, but--even as is the case among men--diversity of tendency and of special vocation.

'Are two notes of the same musical chord unequal or of different nature? Man and woman are the two notes without which the Human chord is impossible. They fulfil different functions in Humanity, but these functions are equally sacred, equally manifestations of that Thought of God which He has made the soul of the universe.

'Consider woman, therefore, as the partner and companion, not merely of your joys and sorrows, but of your thoughts, your aspirations, your studies, and your endeavors after social amelioration. Consider her your equal in your civil and political life. Be ye the two human wings that lift the soul towards the Ideal we are destined to attain.'

William Lloyd Garrison, in an introduction to 'Joseph Mazzini, his life, writings, and political principles,' writes:

'Mazzini's concern for the rights of man was never, on any pretext, in a purely masculine sense. Years ago he inculcated the equality of the sexes in regard to all civil and political immunities. Largely indebted to his mother for the grand impulses which led him to consecrate his life to the service of his country, his generic respect for woman amounted almost to sanctitude: it was the embodiment of all that is tender in affection, fragrant in purity, devout in aspiration, and self-sacrificing in love.'

It has never been a matter of much regret to me that so little is known of Shakespeare's personal history--the circumstances of his outer life. Of what his interior life was, we can have no doubt. It must have been a life capable of sympathetically reproducing within itself all the great characters, men and women, of the Dramas. But if I could wear the wishing-cap of Fortunatus, I would wish to know what manner of woman, in all particulars, was Mary Arden, the poet's mother. The men whose intellectual and, more especially, spiritual gifts to the world, have been the greatest, and most quickening, have oftener, no doubt, been more indebted, for those gifts, to their mothers than to their fathers. The radiant shapes of the women of Shakespeare's Dramas certainly had their source in the feminine element, the ewig weibliche, of his nature, and this element was as certainly, I cannot but think, derived from, and quickened by, his mother. In what was, without doubt, his earliest play, Love's Labor's Lost, Biron, I am quite sure, expresses Shakespeare's own opinion of the peculiar power of women (A. IV. S. III.):

From women's eyes this doctrine I derive: They sparkle still the right

Promethean fire; They are the books, the arts, the academes, That show, contain, and nourish all the world.

This was as certainly Shakespeare's own opinion about woman as what Biron says (A. I. S. I.) was his own opinion about study:

Study is like the heaven's glorious sun, That will not be deep-search'd with saucy looks; Small have continual plodders ever won, Save base authority from others' books. These earthly godfathers of heaven's lights, That give a name to every fixed star, Have no more profit of their shining nights Than those that walk and wot not what they are. Too much to know is to know nought but fame; And every godfather can give a name.

Shakespeare must early have felt his superiority in true education (the nimble play of all the faculties) to the merely learned men with whom he came in contact, and must soon have discovered that he drank from fountains of which they knew nothing. His own vitality of soul was responsive to the essential life of men and things; and it was through this responsiveness that he attained to a wisdom inaccessible to mere learning and intellectual enlightenment. It was his mother, I like to think, who initiated him into the mysteries of the spirit.

###